Dark Eyes
and
Other Poems

R. UDAYA BHANU

PARTRIDGE
A Penguin Random House Company

To order additional copies of this book, contact
Toll Free 800 101 2657 (Singapore)
Toll Free 1 800 81 7340 (Malaysia)
orders.singapore@partridgepublishing.com
www.partridgepublishing.com/singapore

DEDICATION

DEDICATED TO ALL THOSE LOVELY SOULS
WHO LOVED AND ADMIRED MY POEMS

The Breeze

When the breeze blows
the curtain sways.
A lovely apparition
delights my expectation.

My vigilance unpaid
yet I'm duty bound.
With unceasing hunger
my soul yearns for her.

The cool breeze welcomes
the uninvited rain.
The window panes protects
the swaying curtain.

She stares at me
with her dark eyes.
A thousand secrets
they tend to convey.

Behold that swelling bosom
a furnace of melting passion.
The chalky window panes
conceal the saucy smiles.

I sweat:—
The virgin fades
with the breeze.
The rain witnessed!

The Nuptial Night

Tender is the night.
The ravishing bride
in gold and crimson
lies on the taffeta
laden with Jasmine.

The full-moon smiles
at her meekness.
She trembles at his footsteps.
The lights fade away
as the fragrance of the joss-sticks linger.
She squeals at his grip.
Her lips are moisturized.
The nuptial apparel drops.
The rays falling on her bare bosom
cast a shadow.

The age-old treasure
is looted under pressure.
Nectar flows to fill
the nuptial night
with blood and sweat.

An Ode to A Loved One

Could acquaintance really
bloom into intense love?
If that be so
ours was too late.
But it is never so.

Breeze that whorl your hair
onto my face emits
fragrance of Springtime love
and the sweet sensation of transient joy.

It's aching to leave you
to go on an academic picnic,
far across the seven seas
where my mind pictures you
as my fair seraph.

Blue hills, green vales,
sounding cataracts and misty tufts;
Eyes of twilight,
You—alas! An ornament
of the East and West.

The Smile

When you smiled,
there was solitude all around.
But to me
it was a telegraphic message.

Clandestine though coquettish,
like a waning moon
canopied by a velvety cloud.
The smile registered again!

I knew what you meant
But lady!
It never hurts even
if you make it known.

Reticence!
I defy you for your pigheadedness.
But at your shyness,
I become a cherry on cocktail.

Death

Today's rage
is the hazel-eyed blonde.
Yesterday she was mismanaged
with Rum and Coke.

Death is like adding
Cordial to Gin.
It makes Creation
complete, poetic and superlative.

Returning After Death

With birth there is misery.
Death ends that worthless struggle
for which you were born.
A struggle that has no meaning
but regret and sorrow
sprinkled with joyless joy.
You elbow others to get to the top
only to see you crumble
and turn into hot ashes
or to decay and rot
and be consumed by maggots.
You glow to see a baby born
but you defy death to see a near one go.
The babe cries for it knows
the vicious world
it has come to.
But the corpse smiles for it knows

the vicious world
has come to an abrupt end.
Death comes in many ways,
but the obituaries always
say as peaceful
and not in pieces.
Dead men tell no tales
and carry no tales thereafter
to confirm about Hell and Heaven.
Pain and pleasure are all here.
Do the dead return
as souls in another body?
Yes, they do.
They do to realize their dreams.

Sensations

The band snaps
and the baby wriggles
as the bare fingers cup
the holy.

Sensation sweet.
A frothy mouth
and edentate.
Unquenchable thirst . . .

Purple orgasm
etches like mildews
on everything placid.
Flashy flushes.

Not erotic . . . .
. . . . but celestial.
Turns lilac
again with sensational cubes.

And Again On Christmas Day

Segregated by slavish teenage,
met on Holy Noel
the gift of pimpled adolescence
is a virgin's sublime love.
Barren branches growing out
of white winter attire
now jeweled with blossoms
remind me of you, Love.
Christmas carols again.
Aroma of sweet wine,
maxi-clad fair lassie
in my arms with effervescence.

Conception

The rutting season robed in rosy hue
has come with a slice of life.
Moments of sweetness
are no more aesthetic.
To do and die in vigour and vitality.

Pepper and salt nourish the sapling.
It grows,
yet unseen by the season.

A sojourn for concupiscence.
Relieved with labour pain.
Chops and gravy flow,
warm and bloody.

Andhra Pickles

Red red capsicum
sour and bitter
but when salted
sweetens.

Brown brown capsicum
juicy and jelly
but when decoloured
waters.

Dark dark capsicum
meshy and seedy
but when tasted
burns both ends.

Cheap Popularity

Popularity,
how disgusting are you!
Why should you stoop
to cheapen sweet girls?

Like a goldfish trapped
in a waterless aquarium,
they wriggle and rot
in your cheap garments.

Noble Popularity,
shun your cheap attire
and let the senseless cocoons
fledge into flamboyant butterflies.

A Love Poem

This evening is but a memory
of yesterday's democratic sex-act.
Those inviting lips at dusk
were in satin glow
sighing for an orgasm.
In Kama-Sutra style
She clawed at me.
I, her Kama Deva
tonight and every night!

The Day When You

The day when you
smiled at me,
I felt the freshness
of a new-born daisy.
Your graceful hugs
coupled with frank invitations
gave a new lease of life
to my bleeding heart.

The day when you
confessed to me,
I felt my ravished love
regaining its virginity.
Your flawless purity
of the white lilies,
balmed my morbid heart-break
to a soothing heart-ache.

The day when you
lay beside me
I felt the innocent warmth
of the rising sun.
Your dark fragrant hair
that brushed against my face,
sent orgasmic complexes
to my dry dying soul.

Proficiency In Physics

When the festive hall echoed her name,
the Max-Factored lady
in her sapphire chiffon saree ascended.
The vermilion on her forehead
like the flowers of May,
smiled in serenity
as she received her award for Physics.

Applause, and a flash too!
The ribboned Physics-text
swelled with pride
when it saddled on her breast
of the would-be bride.

Death Again

That laceration
you inflicted on me
could never heal
with all your antibiotics.

Your laser-ray eyes
which penetrated me
proved an elixir
to my ageing muscles.

That lip-stick mark
on my sunken cheek
is a green signal
to do and die.

A Date

We stood hand in hand
studying the splashing waves.
Never was the sea so violent
Never was my heart so restless.

We moved under palm trees
just like crabs on rocks.
Never were we so dead tired
Never were our passions so deadly.

We sheltered in a hotel.
Our lips met a thousand times.
Never were you so determined
Never was I so sensational.

Integration

I undergo electrolysis
When I meet her.

I undergo dialysis
When I kiss her.

I undergo osmosis
When I hug her.

Postal Picnic

Go on
slaughtering my soul.
Chisel your nerves
to slice my love.

Devilish designs
stooping towards hell,
malignant ulcers
and momentary favoritism.

The black kernel
of your ruthless machination
maims the succulence
of our amorous intercom.

Halcyon days will come
when you and I unite.
And he pays the price
with his pale blood.

So feast on
with your dirty manipulations.
Go on,
and meet your watery grave.

A Day In May

Let not tension plague me
for I have another hour.
Dying inch by inch before
I meet those dark eyes.

The honeyed dews of May
bless my holy thoughts.
In loneliness I gather myself
Blue Bells, Poppies and Roses.

Our arms locked, lips met!
Swift is the arrow of Cupid.
We freeze!

Symptomatic

Pale
as a dissected worm.
Nausea.
Loss of appetite.
Hyperacidity.
Midnight lotions,
Blue dreams.
Orange poems.
Sleeps with a Dutch wife.
Iced lemonade.
Dazed.
Angina pectoris.
Disease : love
Cause : teenage flea
Treatment : gingered Honey

Sparks

The last three weeks
plagued me with
romantic rheumatism.
Her unusual silence
gelatinized my nerves
and minced me
into a ball of flesh,
lifeless, sinless
yet bleeding
with arterial blood.
She is the very life
throbbing in me.
And without her
life ceases for us.
But this dark grey
haunting indifference
is nightmarish.

It is so,
because I am a man.
Love,
light me up.
Send me a cube of your love
to keep me glowing
with greenish sparks.

What Are You, Love?

Love,
my poppy thoughts ran wild
all over you
to know what you are.

One scarlet eve
when golden spangles of honey dew
drew my body zones closer,
I saw a spectrum of optical illusions
in your dark retina.

Carefree nymph—
My orchestral tissues you numbed
but promising me
another blue hour to sin.
Till then, I know not
what you are.

Darkness

Starless night
drive me deeper
into your devastating darkness.
Youthful shades
in voiceless void.
Icy wild mist sends me
variable idiosyncracies.
Living corpse
undergoing post-mortem
at Lover's park.
Wrap me,
Darkness,
in your yellow fog
and roll me towards dawn.

Fair Statistics

Statistics,
why scald my soul
with your mean modes?

Polygon designs
and devilish correlations
feast on cumulative ulcers.
Why grin,
you thorn in the flesh?
Near is your heavenly interval.

September 78

September rolling in
to set the winking dusk
with sacred neon flashes to ignite
love's choicest beings.

September 78
with her swishing hips
reminds of September lovers
painted on white canvas.

Freedom

Stirring in yellow molten vermilion,
scarlet Kaliyuga mixed with petals of Edelweiss
have started haunting her.
I punctuated those dark eyes
with sandal perfumes in all freedom—
social and moral.
For ages freedom was chained
but today Holy Kaliyuga melted the frost in me
and let the Gods emerge from
the sporadic fire-rains and deluge of Kama.

Love's Epitaph

Among the shady pines
It stood majestically in white marble.
A work of art to throb every heart
Meeting this marble column.
Men had died but not their love
for this is the beginning of an end.
A spirit of yellow mist
and blue diamonds evolved.
It made me a decoction of love.
Vapours of iodine emitted from the column.
My soul left my frame for a nostalgic homage.
I have loved
but not died.
My soul has died
for it had loved.

Love's Woe

The violet twilight of this February
reminds me of the festival of love
we once shared in the grand symphony
of the Bharata Natyam drums.
Green Maxi,
why pierce my soul and make me pine
with your deadly silence?

Love not,
to whirlpool me
but to honey our delicate moments
and gather Rajni Gandhi together.

Through Love's Alley

Flaming through love's tumultuous alley,
I fell and died prematurely
like green wasps racing towards honey comb.
Not till I met her
in her dashing Red Maxi.
I knew how to love
and to love alfresco.

Madras Today

As the innocent azure blue sky
is dipped in vermilion
by the holidaying Sun,
the fair city of Madras holds a promise
So cherishing
So sacred
So sweet
that I never knew there was
So much of innocence
So much of truth
So much of warmth
in her.

Madras today
means everything to me.
Her love is
So precious
So personal

So possessive
that a new life throbs in me.
She is my happiness
and completes my love poem.

She Was Scared

On our first night
we stole velvety minutes
from mercuric hours
to avoid sleepy eye-lids punctuating.
The love spirits
of Plato and Nietzsche
haunted our resolutions
But she was scared.

Kisses vaporized as hours melted.
A fever.
While new hugs overlapped old ones
I whispered.
The organic night was dying out
But she was scared.

Her soul sheltered in my frame
and we became one as she kissed me
in the shady dawn.

As the moment wheel-chaired in
She faded with coyness.
Love,
will I have another silky night
to see you recoil?

Catch Spiders In Their Own Webs

Ill-assorted ignoble iguanas
instigated incautious spiders
to spin impish, immature webs
to impede nature's progress.

So the smarmy spiders
spun silken flaming webs
to wilt flowering nature.
Spiny, stealthy iguanas
ignorant of nature's glory
will be torched by divinity.
They hatched plots against nature.

Unless the same sordid spiders
severe all reptilian ties
they will be caught in their own webs.

My Wounded Conscience

I was left in an ambivalent daze
bordering on a brazen overture.
I was mercilessly persecuted,
killing my intellectual prowess
and searing my soul by injustice.

I fell into decay
of chronic self-absorption,
my desires dissolving in my conscience,
ripping my warped soul open.
Their ribald envy
and bloated ego
cringed me with morbid phobia.
I could have been
a walking stick of dynamite
with the fuse lit.

But my self-esteem confined me
to an inexplicable scornful solidarity.
No peace but everything in pieces.

No equality but the bitter irony—
A malaise, intellectually strangulating
devastated by a giant squid.
Social snobbery locked in neurosis
and violence that led to an orgiastic future.
The self-flagellation of my psyche
is the price I pay for my existence here.
Deranged by extreme grief
and occasional insanity,
I was like King Popiel.
Though the punishment assumed sinister dimensions,
I vigorously championed
my cause for equality.

I knew
morality versus racialism is no contest.
My conscience ruptured
at the impact of their oyster knife.
I was losing grip . . . .
I knew I would not win
but these inglorious men of barbaric instincts
would one day realize the truth—
the truth that we are all equal.
No man deserves pain and torture
inflicted by fellowmen without justice.

Deepa Aradhana

The grand symphony
Of the temple of Attukal
reflects a shade of silken love
in a forgotten melody.
Flow-Pamba-Flow.

The white sandal marks
on my violet Devi
speak of sweet words unsaid.
Souls churn.
Blow-Cape Jasmines-Blow.

I melt into you
as camphor fumes.
The sweet longing
for Manacaud's mascara.
Oil lamps burn out.
Flow-Pamba-Flow.

A noisy festival outside
a silent desire inside.
Shelter me in your dark eyes.
A spray of rose water.
Blow-Cape Jasmines-Blow.

Accept my Deepa Aradhana
and redeem me
from the hot ashes of frost.
Love me once.
Flow-Pamba-Flow.

Speak Devi—
Grant me a thousand births
to be with you forever.
I wait
till sunrise tomorrow.
Blow-Cape Jasmines-Blow.

Paternal Love

A frail furrier father
salves the karmic agonies
of his candy-flossed albinos
by his benignity.
Voices of cosmic unity
strength and sanity.
Visions of universal love,
sanctity and security.
Their feeble pink retinas
reveal febrile filial piety.
Human fledgelings
set aside as rotting haulm
in cold shackles
of a body-conscious Home
can only wallow
in the mellowed richness
of a famed fervent father.

Is It Right For You?

Full of fuming fury,
the dark yawning chasms
of hatred and selfishness
froth a stinking caucus.
Like cyborgs dancing on mars,
they proselytize culpable students—
Chanting an unknown idiom
inciting sporadic arson.

Colourful caps and catapults,
Without disks and dissertations,
Confront cops and water-cannons.

The nation watches and echoes:

Is it right for you
to hold street demonstrations
and throw Molotov cocktails?

Is it right for you
to stamp on a newsman's vehicle
and to stir-fry the national flag?

Is it right for you
to forget the privileges
and create hate crimes?

Is it right for you
to chant anti-government slogans
and to subsist on government loans?

Neither street violence
nor trench coat mafia
is our culture.
We are streetwise.

Caning, Not For Girls

The cane is a good maid but a bad matron.
They use it in the classrooms.
They use it in prisons.
They use it at homes.
They abuse it at the market-squares.
When they put it to disuse,
maniacs, miscreants and monsters
grit their teeth and flex their muscles.
They misused it in the lunatic asylums
to shut away the evil spirits
until Sigmund Freud taught them psychoanalysis.

The cane is a good maid but a bad matron.
It serves as a deterrent
to drug-traffickers and human-traffickers,
kidnappers, rapists and road bullies.

Errant boys are made of tougher stuff,
not that they are thick-skinned
but conditioned at home like Pavlov's dog
by paternal ring-masters.
So once beaten twice shy.

Errant girls tiptoeing into classrooms
in their pony-tails and school uniforms,
in their Cinderella and Snow White images
should not be caned.
They are not monsters, miscreants or maniacs.
Why should the whip or the lash or the cane
be used on errant girls in schools?
Why can't care, compassion and kindness
blossom on school premises?

Teachers with conviction and conscience
will not abuse or misuse the cane
for the one who is caned knows
that the pain lingers long after she feels it no more.

You And Me

Snatch of rhythm
mango shake and cocoa,
yearning for the voice of love,
You and me in the tempo of life.

Sigh of relief
on the island of love.
Cubes of fire in the dark retina,
You and me in sundown fever.

Song of Krishna
almost always true.
Dimpled midnight slashing towards dawn,
You and me in newly-wedded love.

Ceasefire 1989

Stop the ubiquitous wars.
Shelve the nuclear race.
World citizens
Unite, for global peace!

The prelude
to man's destruction
is war—primitive or sophisticated.
War crumbles man's civilization.

Religious fanatics,
parochial paraplagics—
You awaken barbaric instincts
to appease the war gods.
The world is a satanic cauldron
where megalomaniacs
commit heinous crimes
and politicians sing elegies.

Ceasefire!
Let peace emerge.
Make peace!
Keep peace!
Respect the Universal Declaration of Human Rights.

In Search Of Peace

With ghoulish hunger
dark withered hands
delve into the viscera
of hard baked earth
in search of grains.
Their hellish motives,
battered bleeding women
and flattened children
with flailing tiny arms
are all locked in neurosis.
Vibrant human lives rotting
with strangulating political malaise;
the foetus in a dead womb floating.
Why, Bosnia, Rwanda or Somalia?
But will the shudder rip through
the conscience of the UN?

If man cannot defend man—
If man cannot protect man—
Will the fair invisible hands
delve into man's psyche
in search of divine peace?

Life

The Organic Self
penetrates through seismic
divine pulsations
clad in sartorial elegance
but hounds the inner conscience
for metaphysical answers.

The Organic Self
permeates through mesmeric
nebulous parturition
sapped by the decades of decadence
but wriggles in the void of nescience
for a psychedelic caress.

The Organic Self
moulds its somatic
fibre in rhythmic gradation
is a vain puppet show that awes.
Life in all its transience
is but a sporadic inorganic mass.

Enfant Terrible

A mugwump breaks loose
into a chameleon fury
with venomous aggression
and villainous nepotism
to douse
the embers of its monomania.

A reptile
in borrowed derma
performing endymatia
with an odour of sanctity
to please the authority.

Egoistic pest
wriggling in the woodpile
discrediting mellowed intelligence
with a 'holier than thou'
hypocritic contrivance.

Time will stigmatize
the vicious designs.
Time will eulogize
the chivalrous denizens.
Till then, swell in your cankerous cocoon.

(Golden Poet Award 1989—World of Poetry, USA)

Man's Arrogant Immortality

Symbol of power
is shrouded in fear.
A salamander
sallies out of the fire,
whereas a sleuth-hound
sniffs aphrodisiac blood.
The nocturnal weirdie
quenches its insatiate thirst.
Thus ending the revelries
of a generation steeped in prejudice.
A preternatural solemn prevails
over the ruptured aorta.
Actions that denote arrogant immortality
rarely realize the power of death
can reduce man into powerless wrigglers.

While the old physicians
are thumbing through the pharmacopoeia
to arrest death—the phantasmagoria,
man is destroying himself through
greed, false pride and violence.

Papier Mache

A loveless, lovely
lovable
Papier Mache
once on a warm December
pulsated me
to teaspoon her
with the tincture of my love.
So, I sprayed her with rose water
from honeyed paper roses.
Then, I sprinkled her with golden pollens
from the wildest flowers.
And then, placed her
at the adytum of my soul
offering a bunch of edelweiss.
Right then, papier mache
became the liquor of my poems.
She was lifeless—
I slipped life into her.

She was loveless—
I schooled love into her.
She was soulless—
I shared my soul with her.
And Papier Mache?
She eternalized my love.

(Golden Poet Award 1990—World of Poetry, USA)

Dark Eyes

Those two dark dark
glistening eyes
bright and large
stared to condense me
into a golden dew drop
on a blue lotus.

I evolved in the warmth
of your twilight love
into an iota
of rainbow sublimity.

I lingered lonely
in your fair perfumery
till peacock eye-shades twinkled.
Then nursed me with saffron,
honey and star-dust.

Dark Eyes,
the lyrics of my love,
baptize me with your love-potion
and complete my sinless rebirth.
Then, with souls in unison
we glow into Spring-time lovers.

Animals Too Need Love

The brute and the mute
are victimized
by Man the wicked.
They have victualled
him since birth.
He preys and imprisons,
takes to taxidermy.
to beautify his mansions.
He subjects
simians and felines
to atrocious experiments

The flying bird
is trapped
in a claustrophobic cage.
A stray dog is stoned
by impish adolescents.

A fattened cow
is milked dry
and sent to the abattoir.
A stiff bull
sprawled in blood
tells a tale . . . .
An automobile accident?
No, an inhuman incident.

The brute is a mute,
yet it has feelings.
It can love, retaliate
and reciprocate.
Man, do you realize
that animals too need love?
Animals have contributed
to the ecology,
flora and fauna
and YOU.
Man,
stop that ruthless annihilation
of a marvelous creation
for animals too need your love.

Kannadasan's Poetry

His poetic repertoire enshrines
the world of spiritual delicacy
in romance, morals and philosophy
of the Tamil celluloid industry.

The songs that Sivaji and MGR sang,
the songs that TMS and Susheela sang,
the songs that M.S. Visvanathan tuned,
the songs that every Indian internalized,
were those that Kannadasan crafted.

His lyrical outbursts
did poetic justice
to create a new genre
in the Tamil film industry.

Poetry that is lofty,
trenchant and mesmerizing—

Poetry that is catchy,
therapeutic and witty—

Poetry that has art,
wisdom and sentiment—

Poetry that has grace,
vision and memories—

Was it Emily or the Muse
who pulsated those divine lyrics?
Lyrics that sensitized
the mind, body and spirit
of the Tamil film industry.

Will Brahma recreate this mould?

(Awarded Grand Prize by ASTRO National Poetry-Writing Contest 2007)

You Will Carry Me Inside Of You

Cloudy skies and summer clouds
capsized a narrow rowing boat
mercilessly throwing a pregnant mother
into the wild gushing waters
of the swift silver river.

The cooing of an unborn
"You are carrying me inside of you"
evoked the merciful Goddess of Water
to drift her to the steps marble
of an ancient Chinese temple.

Four months later
saved by the holy Ganges water
the 13th child Gangadharan
was born as Jeganathan.

Seven months later
with divinity in her soul
religion in her heart
raga on her lips
Jega on her hips
as a social icon she emerged
singing and preaching—
sacrificing as a single glowing candle.

She fed us
when we were hungry
She cheered us
when we were unhappy
She nursed us
when we were sickly.
At eight
I lay my restless head
on my mother's lap.
At eighty-eight
my mother lay her restful head
on my lap.

Tonight
amidst cocktail, poetry and magic
we celebrate
the warmth and strength
of an 88 old devoted mother
whose cherishing memory
Is treasured in a biography
by the Lord of the Universe.
Once I cooed unborn
"You are carrying me inside of you".
Today from Kashmir to Kamunting
"I carry you inside of me"
till my corporal frame
is consumed by the flame
and reincarnated to echo
"You will carry me inside of you
from yuga to yuga
as your Jega".

Let's Celebrate The Nation's Success Story

56 years of sacrifices
tears, tempers and triumphs
have preserved the dignity,
sovereignty and unity
of this unique land
that I call my native land.

The beaming bubbly populace
that practises tolerance
has enabled this golden land
to uphold guided democracy
with peace and prosperity
flowing freely in harmony.

My native land is divinely devoid
of devilish volcanic eruptions,
devastating hellish hurricanes
and devious earthquakes.

So, our leaders past and present
have made her a haven
even for others
to call her their second home.

Our walk the talk Prime Minister does vow
People First, Performance Now.
Fairness and freedom are enshrined in 1Malaysia,
Single mothers and pensioners are enriched by BR1M.
Here things are not grim
when comfort is up to your brim.

Transformation is wiping out where
bribery, dishonesty and poverty exist.
Don't turn our Dataran Merdeka
into a Tahrir or Tiananmen Square
for when we are blessed with sight
the value of our eyes we tend to forget.

The I-pad kids of today have a field day
as Merdeka Day is just another public holiday.
They do not have the same sentiments
as we had when we were radio kids.
And as we celebrate we wonder
whether patriotism is placed on the back burner?

So, celebrate the success story of our land.
Let hands flutter the Jalur Gemilang
and hearts render the NegaraKu
in line with the echoes sounded by Tunku.

Celebrating Malaysia's Golden Anniversary

As we celebrate Malaysia's
50th anniversary with a clear conscience
How many of us can reminisce
the dreams and diligence
of those who adeptly without bloodshed
created a watershed
by uniting Malaya, Sarawak and Sabah.

Though the South China Sea
was seen as a difficult divide,
Kuala Lumpur, Kuching and Kota Kinabalu
became a trinity of mutual trust and peace.
Our leaders and rakyats proved
Malaysia Boleh in 1963.

The initial querulous stumbling blocks
were quickly sanctified into stepping stones.

Despite a myriad of cultures and festivals
development was on the fast lane.
The longest bridge, a 2020 airport, the tallest towers,
and the nation's signature cars
are all but striking and stunning realities.

Our fallen heroes
and our unsung heroes
are all a tribute to our golden nation.
Insurgents and secret societies
are decimated by *Op Cantas*.
Abject poverty is not an excuse
to join insidious gangs.
Isn't this a nation full of opportunities
where even immigrants eke out a living?
To live here as citizens
and to bellyache about dire poverty is a crime.

Elected leaders should uplift their own community.
"Be fair, right and equitable", says our Prime Minister.
This will solve the unfairness, the wrong and the inequality.
No public servant should be a mudslinger
after 50 years of peace, prosperity and public service.
Do not bite or chew the hand
that has fed us for 50 years.

Seeking One World Through Poetry

If people were of one colour
Will there be racial discrimination?
If people were of one religion
Will they be united with each other?
If people had plenty in the granary
Will they be hungry?
If people were all healthy
Will there be apothecaries?
If people were all wealthy
Will there be break-ins?
If people were all activists
Will they all be arrivistes?
If people were all beautiful
Will there be beauty contests?
If people were all followers
Will there be leaders?
If people respected the environment
Will there be natural disasters?

If people are all takers
Will there be any givers?
If people are all singers
Will there be any listeners?
If people are all arrogant
Will there be a humble pie to eat?
If people were all righteous
Will there be prisons?
If people were all citizens of the world
Will there be narrow parochialism?
If only people were contented
Our world will be heavenly.
One world without crime, drugs and war.
One world without terrorism.
One world without nuclear threat
But one world through poetry.

Loving Care For All Children

While we revel
in technological advances,
the strident voice
of malnutrition
that begs for a morsel
hits us like shrapnel
to paralyse
the psycho-socio onslaught
on Children.
We exploit child labour
and never harbour
the homeless.
We deprive them
of a life of their own
and never protect them
from armed conflicts
and preventable maladies.

The survival of these divine beings
rests on the fruits of the World Summit.
Can the World Summit for Children
love, care and develop Children
with paternal protection
and maternal affection?

A Plea On Earth Day

Man,
in your struggle
for opulence, power and procreation,
have you not culled
the anatomy of the Earth?

Man,
you carve cubicles
to ensconce yourself in—
have you not in
abundance procreated
with no victuals for the future?

Man,
you stifle the Earth's lungs
by your greenhouse effect—
her nostrils swell
to see a hole in the skies
made by ozone depleting chemicals.

Man,
The Earth is running a temperature!
Her systems are failing,
yet you gnaw away
her degenerating viscera.
The vicissitudes of posterity
are engineered by your technology.

Man,
your ravenous destruction
of the environment
will propel you
to gasp in the Earth's foyer.

Gloomy-faced Earth
persuasively appeals
for the reconciliation of myopic man.
The crowd and pollution
make him a confused-self.

Mother Earth
shall sensitise
and sanitise Man.
She has to impose a carbon tax.
She lulls him to use geothermal energy.

Man,
if you do not sacrifice
future needs,
the Earth would transform
into a colossal coffin
satisfying current needs.

Watching Behind Closed Doors

I relish
my retreat into
the dark niche
of human fatality
and embark on a courtship
with nobody but myself.

My morphology
ruptures your ego
but the more you conceal
the more I reveal.
Your repulsive stares
and callous grins
are only mute innuendoes.

You deprive me, punish me,
and bundle me
off into institutions
to render me useless.

Your warped conscience is shackled,
nailed to a snobbish ritual,
shredded by an insensitive society.

My traumatized cries
for acceptance are never echoed—
Am I a social curse?
Or a genetic aberrant?
I will never know . . . .
Though I drool and dribble
I am not society's silly rigmarole.

Arrant hypocrite,
moulded out of shame and hatred,
you snatch my right to live.
I am not a fiddle-crab
but an entangled mass
floating as society's dross.
I watch behind closed doors
and then commune with myself:
If I were you, and you were me . . . .
Would you still eavesdrop on society?